CONTENTS

D1042944

CLASSIC COLLECTION

Jumbo 3-Chip Cookies

- 4 cups all-purpose flour
- 1 teaspoon baking powder
- 1 teaspoon baking soda
- 1½ cups (3 sticks) butter, softened
- 1¼ cups granulated sugar
- 1¼ cups packed brown sugar
- 2 large eggs
- 1 tablespoon vanilla extract
- 1 cup (6 ounces) NESTLÉ® TOLL HOUSE® Milk Chocolate Morsels
- 1 cup (6 ounces) NESTLÉ® TOLL HOUSE® Semi-Sweet Chocolate Morsels
- ½ cup NESTLÉ® TOLL HOUSE® Premier White Morsels
- 1 cup chopped nuts

PREHEAT oven to 375°F.

COMBINE flour, baking powder and baking soda in medium bowl. Beat butter, granulated sugar and brown sugar in large mixer bowl until creamy. Beat in eggs and vanilla extract. Gradually beat in flour mixture. Stir in morsels and nuts. Drop dough by level ¼-cup measure 2 inches apart onto ungreased baking sheets.

BAKE for 12 to 14 minutes or until light golden brown. Cool on baking sheets for 2 minutes; remove to wire racks to cool completely.

Makes about 2 dozen cookies

Milk Chocolate Oatmeal Cookies

- 1¼ **cups all-purpose flour**
- ½ **teaspoon baking powder**
- ½ **teaspoon baking soda**
- ½ **teaspoon ground cinnamon**
- ¼ **teaspoon salt**
- ¾ **cup (1½ sticks) butter or margarine, softened**
- ¾ **cup packed brown sugar**
- ⅓ **cup granulated sugar**
- 1½ **teaspoons vanilla extract**
- 1 **large egg**
- 2 **tablespoons milk**
- 1¾ **cups (11.5-ounce package) NESTLÉ® TOLL HOUSE® Milk Chocolate Morsels**
- 1 **cup quick or old-fashioned oats**
- ½ **cup raisins (optional)**

PREHEAT oven to 375°F.

COMBINE flour, baking powder, baking soda, cinnamon and salt in small bowl. Beat butter, brown sugar, granulated sugar and vanilla extract in large mixer bowl until creamy. Beat in egg. Gradually beat in flour mixture and milk. Stir in morsels, oats and raisins. Drop by rounded tablespoon onto ungreased baking sheets.

BAKE for 10 to 14 minutes or until edges are crisp but centers are still soft. Cool on baking sheets for 2 minutes; remove to wire racks to cool completely.

Makes about 3 dozen cookies

Quick Tiramisu

1 package (16.5 ounces) NESTLÉ® TOLL HOUSE®
 Refrigerated Sugar Cookie Bar Dough
¾ teaspoon NESCAFÉ® TASTER'S CHOICE® House
 Blend 100% Pure Instant Coffee Granules
¾ cup cold water
1 package (8 ounces) ⅓ less fat cream cheese
 (Neufchâtel) at room temperature
½ cup granulated sugar
1 container (8 ounces) frozen whipped topping, thawed
1 tablespoon NESTLÉ® TOLL HOUSE® Baking Cocoa

PREHEAT oven to 325°F.

CUT cookie dough into 20 pieces. Shape each piece into a 2½×1-inch oblong
 shape. Place on ungreased baking sheets.

BEAT for 10 to 12 minutes or until light golden brown around edges. Cool on
 baking sheets for 1 minute; remove to wire racks to cool completely.

DISSOLVE coffee granules in cold water; set aside.

BEAT cream cheese and sugar in large mixer bowl until smooth. Beat in ¼ cup
 coffee. Fold in whipped topping. Layer 6 cookies in ungreased 8-inch-square
 baking dish. Sprinkle each cookie with *1 teaspoon* coffee. Spread *one-third*
 cream cheese mixture over cookies. Repeat layers 2 more times with *12*
 cookies, *remaining* coffee and *remaining* cream cheese mixture. Cover;
 refrigerate for 2 to 3 hours. Crumble *remaining* cookies over top. Sift cocoa
 over cookies. Cut into squares.

Makes 12 servings

Stained Glass Window Cookies

1 package (16.5 ounces) **NESTLÉ® TOLL HOUSE®**
 Refrigerated Sugar Cookie Bar Dough
 All-purpose flour
 About ½ cup finely crushed hard candy

PREHEAT oven to 325°F. Line baking sheets with foil.

CUT dough in half; refrigerate one half. Sprinkle about 1 tablespoon flour onto working surface. Sprinkle additional flour over *remaining* half. Roll out dough to ¼-inch thickness, using additional flour as needed to prevent sticking.

CUT into desired shapes with 2½-inch cookie cutters. Transfer cookies to prepared baking sheets with spatula, placing about 2 inches apart. Cut out small shapes in cookie centers. Spoon candy into each center to fill holes. Pierce hole at top of shape if cookie is going to be hung. Repeat with remaining dough.

BAKE for 8 to 11 minutes or until edges are light golden brown. Cool on baking sheets for 1 minute; slide foil with cookies to wire racks to cool completely. Store in airtight container.

Makes 20 cookies

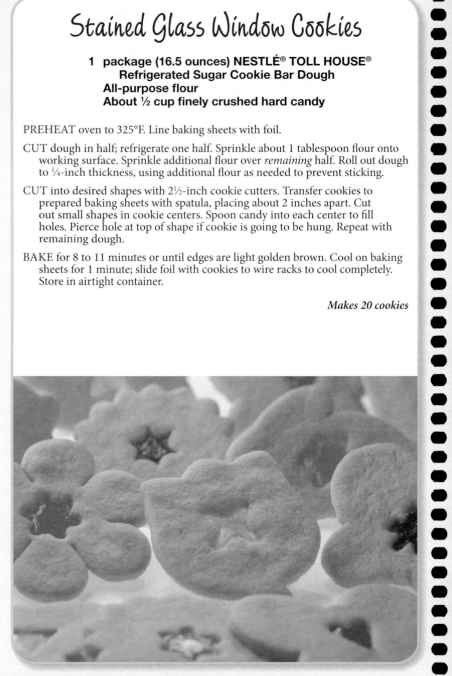

Orange Brunch Muffins

- 3 cups all-purpose baking mix
- ¾ cup all-purpose flour
- ⅔ cup granulated sugar
- 2 large eggs, lightly beaten
- ½ cup plain yogurt
- ½ cup orange juice
- 1 tablespoon grated orange peel
- 2 cups (12-ounce package) NESTLÉ® TOLL HOUSE® Premier White Morsels, *divided*
- ½ cup chopped macadamia nuts or walnuts

PREHEAT oven to 375°F. Grease or paper-line 18 muffin cups.

COMBINE baking mix, flour and sugar in large bowl. Add eggs, yogurt, orange juice and orange peel; stir just until blended. Stir in *1⅓ cups* morsels. Spoon into prepared muffin cups, filling ¾ full. Sprinkle with nuts.

BAKE for 18 to 22 minutes or until wooden pick inserted in centers comes out clean. Cool in pans for 10 minutes; remove to wire racks to cool slightly.

MICROWAVE *remaining ⅓ cup* morsels in small, *heavy-duty* plastic bag on MEDIUM-HIGH (70%) power for 1 minute; knead. Microwave at additional 10- to 15-second intervals, kneading until smooth. Cut tiny corner from bag; squeeze to drizzle over muffins. Serve warm.

Makes 18 muffins

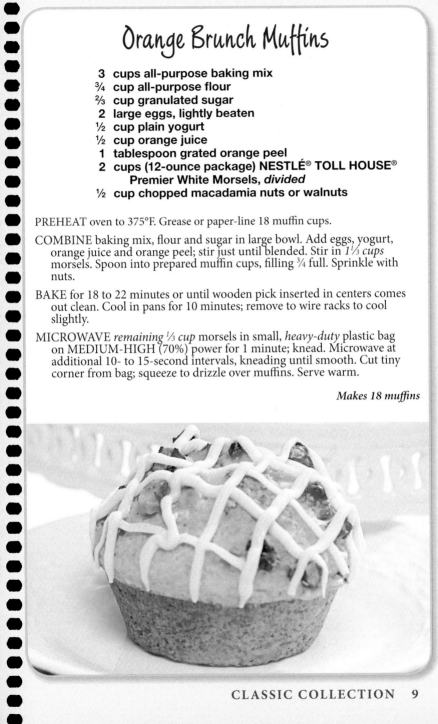

Double Chocolate Warm Pudding Cake

Nonstick cooking spray
1 cup all-purpose flour
1¼ cups granulated sugar, *divided*
3 tablespoons *plus* ¼ cup NESTLÉ® TOLL HOUSE®
  Baking Cocoa, *divided*
2 teaspoons baking powder
¼ teaspoon salt
1 can (12 fluid ounces) NESTLÉ® CARNATION®
  Evaporated Lowfat 2% Milk, *divided*
1 tablespoon vegetable oil
1 teaspoon vanilla extract
2 tablespoons water
Lowfat whipped topping or ice cream (optional)

PREHEAT the oven to 350° F. Spray 8-inch-square baking pan or dish with nonstick cooking spray.

COMBINE flour, ¾ cup sugar, *3 tablespoons* cocoa, baking powder and salt in medium bowl. Add ½ cup evaporated milk, oil and vanilla extract; whisk until just blended. Spread batter into prepared baking pan.

COMBINE *remaining ½ cup* sugar and ¼ cup cocoa in small bowl. Microwave *remaining 1 cup* evaporated milk and water in small, uncovered microwave-safe bowl on HIGH (100%) power for 1 minute. Whisk sugar-cocoa mixture into milk mixture until blended. Gently pour over chocolate batter in pan.

BAKE for 20 to 25 minutes (25 to 30 minutes if using glass dish) or until cake layer forms on top and edges are bubbly. Let stand for 10 minutes. Spoon into serving dishes, spooning chocolate sauce over cake. Top with whipped topping.

Tip: *Individual servings can be reheated in microwave for 10 seconds.*

Makes 9 servings

Old-Fashioned Lemon Bread

- 1½ cups all-purpose flour
- 1 cup granulated sugar
- 1 teaspoon baking powder
- ½ teaspoon salt
- 2 large eggs
- ⅔ cup (5 fluid-ounce can) NESTLÉ® CARNATION® Evaporated Milk
- ⅓ cup olive or vegetable oil
- 1½ teaspoons grated lemon peel (about 1 lemon— reserve lemon for later use)
- Lemon Syrup (recipe follows)

PREHEAT oven to 350°F. Grease and flour 8×4-inch baking pan.

COMBINE flour, sugar, baking powder and salt in large bowl. Beat eggs, evaporated milk, oil and lemon zest together in medium bowl. Pour egg mixture into flour mixture. Stir until just combined. Pour into prepared pan.

BAKE for 55 to 60 minutes or until wooden skewer inserted in center comes out clean. Using the skewer, poke numerous holes in the hot bread, piercing all the way to the bottom. Slowly drizzle the hot Lemon Syrup over the bread (Syrup will soak into the bread). Cool on wire rack for 15 minutes; run knife around edge of bread. Remove bread to wire rack to cool completely.

Makes 1 loaf (10 servings)

Lemon Syrup: COMBINE ⅓ cup granulated sugar and ¼ cup lemon juice (1 lemon) in small, heavy-duty saucepan. Cook over medium-low heat, stirring constantly, for about 5 minutes or until sugar is dissolved and a light syrup is formed.

Donna's Heavenly Orange Chip Scones

  4 cups all-purpose flour
  1 cup granulated sugar
  4 teaspoons baking powder
  ½ teaspoon baking soda
  ½ teaspoon salt
  1 cup (6 ounces) NESTLÉ® TOLL HOUSE® Semi-Sweet
    Chocolate Mini Morsels
  1 cup golden raisins
  1 tablespoon grated orange peel
  1 cup (2 sticks) unsalted butter, cut into pieces and
    softened
  1 cup buttermilk
  3 large eggs, *divided*
  1 teaspoon orange extract
  1 tablespoon milk
    Icing (recipe follows)

PREHEAT oven to 350°F. Lightly grease baking sheets.

COMBINE flour, granulated sugar, baking powder, baking soda and salt in large
bowl. Add morsels, raisins and orange peel; mix well. Cut in butter with
pastry blender or 2 knives until mixture resembles coarse crumbs. Combine
buttermilk, 2 eggs and orange extract in small bowl. Pour buttermilk mixture
into flour mixture; mix just until a sticky dough is formed. Do not overmix.
Drop by ¼ cupfuls onto prepared baking sheets. Combine *remaining* egg and
milk in small bowl. Brush egg mixture over top of dough.

BAKE for 18 to 22 minutes or until wooden pick inserted in center comes out
clean. For best results, bake one baking sheet at a time. Cool on wire racks for
10 minutes. Drizzle scones with Icing. Serve warm.

Makes 2 dozen scones

Icing: COMBINE 2 cups powdered sugar, ¼ cup orange juice, 1 tablespoon
*grated orange peel and 1 teaspoon orange extract in medium bowl. Mix
until smooth.*

Milk Chocolate Florentine Cookies

- ⅔ cup butter
- 2 cups quick oats
- 1 cup granulated sugar
- ⅔ cup all-purpose flour
- ¼ cup light or dark corn syrup
- ¼ cup milk
- 1 teaspoon vanilla extract
- ¼ teaspoon salt
- 1¾ cups (11.5-ounce package) NESTLÉ® TOLL HOUSE® Milk Chocolate Morsels

PREHEAT oven to 375°F. Line baking sheets with foil.

MELT butter in medium saucepan; remove from heat. Stir in oats, sugar, flour, corn syrup, milk, vanilla extract and salt; mix well. Drop by level teaspoon, about 3 inches apart, onto foil-lined baking sheets. Spread thinly with rubber spatula.

BAKE for 6 to 8 minutes or until golden brown. Cool completely on baking sheets on wire racks. Peel foil from cookies.

MICROWAVE morsels in medium, uncovered, microwave-safe bowl on MEDIUM-HIGH (70%) power for 1 minute. STIR. Morsels may retain some of their original shape. If necessary, microwave at additional 10- to 15-second intervals, stirring just until morsels are melted. Spread thin layer of melted chocolate onto flat side of *half* the cookies. Top with *remaining* cookies.

Makes about 3½ dozen sandwich cookies

Oatmeal Scotchies

- 1¼ **cups all-purpose flour**
- 1 **teaspoon baking soda**
- ½ **teaspoon salt**
- ½ **teaspoon ground cinnamon**
- 1 **cup (2 sticks) butter or margarine, softened**
- ¾ **cup granulated sugar**
- ¾ **cup packed brown sugar**
- 2 **large eggs**
- 1 **teaspoon vanilla extract *or* grated peel of 1 orange**
- 3 **cups quick or old-fashioned oats**
- 1⅔ **cups (11-ounce package) NESTLÉ® TOLL HOUSE® Butterscotch Flavored Morsels**

PREHEAT oven to 375°F.

COMBINE flour, baking soda, salt and cinnamon in small bowl. Beat butter, granulated sugar, brown sugar, eggs and vanilla extract in large mixer bowl. Gradually beat in flour mixture. Stir in oats and morsels. Drop by rounded tablespoon onto ungreased baking sheets.

BAKE for 7 to 8 minutes for chewy cookies or 9 to 10 minutes for crisp cookies. Cool on baking sheets for 2 minutes; remove to wire racks to cool completely.

Makes about 4 dozen cookies

Pan Cookie Variation: *GREASE 15×10-inch jelly-roll pan. Prepare dough as above. Spread into prepared pan. Bake for 18 to 22 minutes or until light brown. Cool completely in pan on wire rack.*

Makes 4 dozen bars.

LIBBY'S® Famous Pumpkin Pie

- ¾ **cup granulated sugar**
- 1 **teaspoon ground cinnamon**
- ½ **teaspoon salt**
- ½ **teaspoon ground ginger**
- ¼ **teaspoon ground cloves**
- 2 **large eggs**
- 1 **can (15 ounces) LIBBY'S® 100% Pure Pumpkin**
- 1 **can (12 fluid ounces) NESTLÉ® CARNATION® Evaporated Milk**
- 1 *unbaked* **9-inch (4-cup volume) deep-dish pie shell Whipped cream (optional)**

MIX sugar, cinnamon, salt, ginger and cloves in small bowl. Beat eggs in large bowl. Stir in pumpkin and sugar-spice mixture. Gradually stir in evaporated milk.

POUR into pie shell.

BAKE in preheated 425°F oven for 15 minutes. Reduce oven temperature to 350°F; bake for 40 to 50 minutes or until knife inserted near center comes out clean. Cool on wire rack for 2 hours. Serve immediately or refrigerate. Top with whipped cream before serving.

Makes 8 servings

Note: *Do not freeze this pie because this will result in the crust separating from the filling.*

Tip: *You can substitute 1¾ teaspoons pumpkin pie spice for the cinnamon, ginger and cloves; however, the flavor will be slightly different.*

For 2 shallow pies: *Substitute two 9-inch (2-cup volume) pie shells. Bake in preheated 425°F oven for 15 minutes. Reduce temperature to 350°F; bake for 20 to 30 minutes or until pies test done.*

VERY BEST BARS

Chocolate Crumb Bars

- 1 cup (2 sticks) butter or margarine, softened
- 1¾ cups all-purpose flour
- ½ cup granulated sugar
- ¼ teaspoon salt
- 2 cups (12-ounce package) NESTLÉ® TOLL HOUSE® Semi-Sweet Chocolate Morsels, *divided*
- 1 can (14 ounces) NESTLÉ® CARNATION® Sweetened Condensed Milk
- 1 teaspoon vanilla extract
- 1 cup chopped walnuts (optional)

PREHEAT oven to 350°F. Grease 13×9-inch baking pan.

BEAT butter in large mixer bowl until creamy. Beat in flour, sugar and salt until crumbly. With floured fingers, press *2 cups* crumb mixture onto bottom of prepared baking pan; reserve *remaining* mixture. BAKE for 10 to 12 minutes or until edges are golden brown.

COMBINE *1 cup* morsels and sweetened condensed milk in small, *heavy-duty* saucepan. Warm over low heat, stirring until smooth. Stir in vanilla extract. Spread over hot crust.

STIR nuts and *remaining* morsels into *reserved* crumb mixture; sprinkle over chocolate filling. Bake for 25 to 30 minutes or until center is set. Cool in pan on wire rack.

Makes 2½ dozen bars

Premier Cheesecake Cranberry Bars

- 2 cups all-purpose flour
- 1½ cups quick or old-fashioned oats
- ¼ cup packed light brown sugar
- 1 cup (2 sticks) butter or margarine, softened
- 2 cups (12-ounce package) NESTLÉ® TOLL HOUSE® Premier White Morsels
- 1 package (8 ounces) cream cheese, softened
- 1 can (14 ounces) NESTLÉ® CARNATION® Sweetened Condensed Milk
- ¼ cup lemon juice
- 1 teaspoon vanilla extract
- 1 can (14 ounces) whole-berry cranberry sauce
- 2 tablespoons cornstarch

PREHEAT oven to 350°F. Grease 13×9-inch baking pan.

COMBINE flour, oats and brown sugar in large bowl. Add butter; mix until crumbly. Stir in morsels. Reserve *2½ cups* morsel mixture for topping. With floured fingers, press *remaining* mixture into prepared pan.

BEAT cream cheese in large mixer bowl until creamy. Add sweetened condensed milk, lemon juice and vanilla extract; mix until smooth. Pour over crust. Combine cranberry sauce and cornstarch in medium bowl. Spoon over cream cheese mixture. Sprinkle *reserved* morsel mixture over cranberry mixture.

BAKE for 35 to 40 minutes or until center is set. Cool completely in pan on wire rack. Cover; refrigerate until serving time (up to 1 day). Cut into bars.

Makes 2½ dozen bars

Swirled Peanut Butter Chocolate Cheesecake Bars

CRUST

- 2 cups graham cracker crumbs
- ½ cup (1 stick) butter or margarine, melted
- ⅓ cup granulated sugar

FILLING

- 2 packages (8 ounces *each*) cream cheese, softened
- 1 cup granulated sugar
- ¼ cup all-purpose flour
- 1 can (12 fluid ounces) NESTLÉ® CARNATION® Evaporated Milk
- 2 large eggs
- 1 tablespoon vanilla extract
- 1 cup (6 ounces) NESTLÉ® TOLL HOUSE® Peanut Butter & Milk Chocolate Morsels

PREHEAT oven to 325°F.

FOR CRUST

COMBINE graham cracker crumbs, butter and sugar in medium bowl; press onto bottom of ungreased 13×9-inch baking pan.

FOR FILLING

BEAT cream cheese, sugar and flour in large mixer bowl until smooth. Gradually beat in evaporated milk, eggs and vanilla extract.

MICROWAVE morsels in medium, uncovered, microwave-safe bowl on MEDIUM–HIGH (70%) power for 1 minute; STIR. The morsels may retain some of their original shape. If necessary, microwave at additional 10- to 15-second intervals, stirring just until melted. Stir *1 cup* cream cheese mixture into chocolate. Pour *remaining* cream cheese mixture over crust. Pour chocolate mixture over cream cheese mixture. Swirl mixtures with spoon, pulling plain cream cheese mixture up to surface.

BAKE for 40 to 45 minutes or until set. Cool completely in pan on wire rack; refrigerate until firm. Cut into bars.

Makes 15 bars

Lemon Cheesecake Bars

- 2 cups all-purpose flour
- ½ cup powdered sugar
- 1 cup (2 sticks) butter, softened
- 1 package (8 ounces) cream cheese, softened
- 2 large eggs
- ⅔ cup (5 fluid-ounce can) NESTLÉ® CARNATION® Evaporated Milk
- ½ cup granulated sugar
- 1 tablespoon all-purpose flour
- 1 tablespoon lemon juice
- 2 teaspoons grated lemon peel
- 1 teaspoon yellow food coloring (optional)
- 1 cup sour cream

PREHEAT oven to 350°F.

COMBINE flour and powdered sugar in medium bowl. Cut in butter with pastry blender or two knives until crumbly. Press onto bottom and 1-inch up sides of ungreased 13×9-inch baking pan.

BAKE for 25 minutes.

PLACE cream cheese, eggs, evaporated milk, granulated sugar, flour, lemon juice, lemon peel and food coloring in blender container; cover. Blend until smooth. Pour into partially baked crust.

BAKE for additional 15 minutes or until set. Cool in pan on wire rack. Spread sour cream over top; refrigerate. Cut into bars. Garnish as desired.

Makes 2 dozen bars

Chocolatey Peanut Pretzel Bars

2½ cups NESTLÉ® TOLL HOUSE® Refrigerated Chocolate Chip Cookie Tub Dough, *divided*

1½ cups (9 ounces) NESTLÉ® TOLL HOUSE® Semi-Sweet Chocolate Morsels, *divided*

1 cup mini-pretzels (about 1¼ ounces), broken into ½-inch pieces

1 cup honey-roasted peanuts

PREHEAT oven to 350°F. Grease 13×9-inch baking pan.

PLACE *2 cups* dough in prepared pan. Using fingertips, pat dough gently to cover bottom.

SPRINKLE *1 cup* morsels, pretzel pieces and peanuts over dough. Drop 1-inch pieces of *remaining ½ cup* cookie dough over peanuts. Sprinkle with *remaining ½ cup* of morsels and gently press down.

BAKE for 23 to 27 minutes or until browned around edges. Cool completely in pan on wire rack. Cut into bars.

Makes 2 dozen bars

Flourless Chocolate Brownies

2 cups (12-ounce package) **NESTLÉ® TOLL HOUSE®** Semi-Sweet Chocolate Morsels, *divided*
¾ cup (1½ sticks) butter, cut into pieces
2 tablespoons water
¼ cup **NESTLÉ® TOLL HOUSE®** Baking Cocoa
4 large eggs
⅓ cup granulated sugar
1 teaspoon vanilla extract
1 cup pecans, finely ground (optional)
¼ cup heavy whipping cream

PREHEAT oven to 300°F. Line 9-inch-square baking pan with foil. Grease bottom and sides.

HEAT 1½ cups morsels, butter and water in medium, *heavy-duty* saucepan over low heat, stirring constantly, until morsels and butter are melted and mixture is smooth. Stir in cocoa until smooth. Remove from heat.

BEAT eggs and sugar in medium mixer bowl until thick, about 4 minutes. Stir in vanilla extract. Fold ⅓ of egg mixture into chocolate mixture. Fold in remaining egg mixture, one half at a time, until thoroughly incorporated. Fold in pecans. Pour into prepared pan.

BAKE for 35 to 40 minutes or until risen in center and edges start to get firm and shiny (center may still move and appear underbaked). Cool completely in pan on wire rack (center may sink slightly). Cover; refrigerate for 4 hours or overnight.

PLACE cream in small, uncovered, microwave-safe dish. Microwave on HIGH (100%) power for 25 to 30 seconds. Add *remaining ½ cup* morsels. Let stand for 2 to 3 minutes; stir until chocolate is melted.

SPREAD ganache over chilled brownie. Refrigerate for 30 minutes. Using two opposite sides of foil, carefully lift the entire brownie out of the pan and place on cutting board. Carefully peel away foil from brownie. Cut into bars. Store in tightly covered container in refrigerator.

Makes 16 brownies

Chocolate Almond Blondie

2½ cups all-purpose flour
1 teaspoon baking soda
1 teaspoon salt
2 cups packed light brown sugar
1 cup (2 sticks) butter, softened
1 teaspoon vanilla extract
2 large eggs
1¾ cups (11.5-ounce package) NESTLÉ®
    TOLL HOUSE® Semi-Sweet Chocolate Chunks,
    divided
1 cup whole almonds, *divided*

PREHEAT oven to 350°F. Grease 13×9-inch baking pan.

COMBINE flour, baking soda and salt in small bowl. Beat brown sugar, butter and vanilla extract in large mixer bowl until creamy. Add eggs; beat until light and fluffy. Gradually stir in flour mixture. Stir in *1 cup* chunks and *½ cup* almonds. Spread into prepared pan. Sprinkle with *remaining* chunks and *½ cup* almonds.

BAKE for 30 to 35 minutes or until golden brown. Cool completely in pan on wire rack. Cut into bars.

Makes 2 dozen bars

No-Bake Chocolate Peanut Butter Bars

- 2 **cups peanut butter,** *divided*
- ¾ **cup (1½ sticks) butter, softened**
- 2 **cups powdered sugar**
- 3 **cups graham cracker crumbs**
- 2 **cups (12-ounce package) NESTLÉ® TOLL HOUSE® Semi-Sweet Chocolate Mini Morsels,** *divided*

GREASE 13×9-inch baking pan.

BEAT *1¼ cups* peanut butter and butter in large mixer bowl until creamy. Gradually beat in *1 cup* powdered sugar. With hands or wooden spoon, work in *remaining* powdered sugar, graham cracker crumbs and ½ *cup* morsels. Press evenly into prepared baking pan. Smooth top with spatula.

MELT *remaining ¾ cup* peanut butter and *remaining 1½ cups* morsels in medium, *heavy-duty* saucepan over *lowest* possible heat, stirring constantly, until smooth. Spread over graham cracker crust in pan. Refrigerate for at least 1 hour or until chocolate is firm. Cut into bars. Store in covered container in refrigerator.

Makes 5 dozen bars

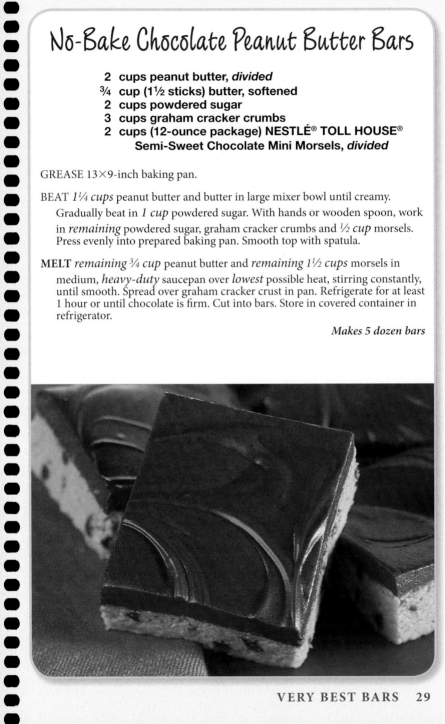

Rocky Road Bars

    2 cups (12-ounce package) NESTLÉ® TOLL HOUSE®
        Semi-Sweet Chocolate Morsels, *divided*
1½ cups all-purpose flour
1½ teaspoons baking powder
    1 cup granulated sugar
    6 tablespoons (¾ stick) butter or margarine, softened
1½ teaspoons vanilla extract
    2 large eggs
    2 cups miniature marshmallows
1½ cups coarsely chopped walnuts

PREHEAT oven to 375°F. Grease 13×9-inch baking pan.

MICROWAVE *1 cup* morsels in medium, uncovered, microwave-safe bowl
   on HIGH (100%) power for 1 minute; STIR. Morsels may retain some of
   their original shape. If necessary, microwave at additional 10- to 15-second
   intervals, stirring just until morsels are melted. Cool to room temperature.
   Combine flour and baking powder in small bowl.

BEAT sugar, butter and vanilla extract in large mixer bowl until crumbly. Beat
   in eggs. Add melted chocolate; beat until smooth. Gradually beat in flour
   mixture. Spread batter into prepared baking pan.

BAKE for 16 to 20 minutes or until wooden pick inserted in center comes out
   slightly sticky.

REMOVE from oven; sprinkle immediately with marshmallows, nuts and
   remaining morsels. Return to oven for 2 minutes or just until marshmallows
   begin to melt. Cool in pan on wire rack for 20 to 30 minutes. Cut into bars
   with wet knife. Serve warm.

Makes 2½ dozen bars

Citrus-Iced Mock Margarita Bars

BAR

- 1 cup *plus* 2 tablespoons all-purpose flour
- 1 teaspoon baking powder
- ¼ teaspoon salt
- ¾ cup granulated sugar
- ⅓ cup butter, softened
- ½ teaspoon vanilla extract
- 2 teaspoons grated lime peel
- 2 teaspoons grated orange peel
- 1 large egg
- 1 cup (6 ounces) NESTLÉ® TOLL HOUSE® Premier White Morsels

CITRUS ICING

- 1½ cups sifted powdered sugar
- 4 ounces cream cheese, at room temperature
- 1 tablespoon butter, softened
- 1 teaspoon grated lime peel
- 1 teaspoon grated orange peel
- 2 teaspoons lime juice
- 1 teaspoon orange juice
- 1 to 2 teaspoons coarse sea salt (optional)

PREHEAT oven to 350°F. Grease 9-inch-square baking pan.

COMBINE flour, baking powder and salt in small bowl. Beat sugar, butter, vanilla extract, lime peel and orange peel in large mixer bowl until creamy. Beat in egg. Gradually beat in flour mixture. Stir in morsels. Press into prepared baking pan.

BAKE for 18 to 20 minutes or until wooden pick inserted in center comes out clean. Cool completely in pan on wire rack. Spread with Citrus Icing. Sprinkle with sea salt. Cut into bars. Store in covered container in refrigerator.

FOR CITRUS ICING

BEAT powdered sugar, cream cheese, butter, lime peel, orange peel, lime juice and orange juice in small mixer bowl until smooth.

Makes 16 bars

Tip: *Bars can be prepared in an 8-inch-square baking pan. Follow recipe above and bake for 20 to 22 minutes.*

BAKING
1-2-3

NESTLÉ® TOLL HOUSE®
Chocolate Chip Pie

- 2 large eggs
- ½ cup all-purpose flour
- ½ cup granulated sugar
- ½ cup packed brown sugar
- ¾ cup (1½ sticks) butter, softened
- 1 cup (6 ounces) NESTLÉ® TOLL HOUSE® Semi-Sweet Chocolate Morsels
- 1 cup chopped nuts
- 1 *unbaked* 9-inch (4-cup volume) deep-dish pie shell*
  Sweetened whipped cream or ice cream (optional)

If using frozen pie shell, use deep-dish style, thawed completely. Bake on baking sheet; increase baking time slightly.

PREHEAT oven to 325°F.

BEAT eggs in large mixer bowl on high speed until foamy. Beat in flour, granulated sugar and brown sugar. Beat in butter. Stir in morsels and nuts. Spoon into pie shell.

BAKE for 55 to 60 minutes or until knife inserted halfway between outside edge and center comes out clean. Cool on wire rack. Serve warm with whipped cream, if desired.

Makes 8 servings

Pumpkin Spiced and Iced Cookies

- 2¼ cups all-purpose flour
- 1½ teaspoons pumpkin pie spice
- 1 teaspoon baking powder
- ½ teaspoon baking soda
- ½ teaspoon salt
- 1 cup (2 sticks) butter or margarine, softened
- 1 cup granulated sugar
- 1 can (15 ounces) LIBBY'S® 100% Pure Pumpkin
- 2 large eggs
- 1 teaspoon vanilla extract
- 2 cups (12-ounce package) NESTLÉ® TOLL HOUSE® Semi-Sweet Chocolate Morsels
- 1 cup chopped walnuts (optional)
  Vanilla Glaze (recipe follows)

PREHEAT oven to 375°F. Grease baking sheets.

COMBINE flour, pumpkin pie spice, baking powder, baking soda and salt in medium bowl. Beat butter and granulated sugar in large mixer bowl until creamy. Beat in pumpkin, eggs and vanilla extract. Gradually beat in flour mixture. Stir in morsels and nuts. Drop by rounded tablespoon onto prepared baking sheets.

BAKE for 15 to 20 minutes or until edges are lightly browned. Cool on baking sheets for 2 minutes; remove to wire racks to cool completely. Drizzle or spread with Vanilla Glaze.

Makes about 5 dozen cookies

Vanilla Glaze: *COMBINE 1 cup powdered sugar, 1 to 1½ tablespoons milk and ½ teaspoon vanilla extract in small bowl; mix well.*

Island Cookies

- 1⅔ cups all-purpose flour
- ¾ teaspoon baking powder
- ½ teaspoon baking soda
- ½ teaspoon salt
- ¾ cup (1½ sticks) butter, softened
- ¾ cup packed brown sugar
- ⅓ cup granulated sugar
- 1 teaspoon vanilla extract
- 1 large egg
- 1¾ cups (11.5-ounce package) NESTLÉ® TOLL HOUSE® Milk Chocolate Morsels
- 1 cup flaked coconut, toasted, if desired
- 1 cup chopped walnuts

PREHEAT oven to 375°F.

COMBINE flour, baking powder, baking soda and salt in small bowl. Beat butter, brown sugar, granulated sugar and vanilla extract in large mixer bowl until creamy. Beat in egg. Gradually beat in flour mixture. Stir in morsels, coconut and nuts. Drop by rounded tablespoon onto ungreased baking sheets.

BAKE for 8 to 11 minutes or until edges are lightly browned. Cool on baking sheets for 2 minutes; remove to wire racks to cool completely.

Makes about 3 dozen cookies

Note: *NESTLÉ® TOLL HOUSE® Semi-Sweet Chocolate Morsels, Semi-Sweet Chocolate Mini Morsels, Premier White Morsels or Butterscotch Flavored Morsels can be substituted for the Milk Chocolate Morsels.*

Double-Chocolate Dream Cookies

2¼ cups all-purpose flour
½ cup **NESTLÉ® TOLL HOUSE®** Baking Cocoa
1 teaspoon baking soda
½ teaspoon salt
1 cup (2 sticks) butter or margarine, softened
1 cup packed brown sugar
¾ cup granulated sugar
1 teaspoon vanilla extract
2 large eggs
2 cups (12-ounce package) **NESTLÉ® TOLL HOUSE®** Semi-Sweet Chocolate Morsels

PREHEAT oven to 375°F.

COMBINE flour, cocoa, baking soda and salt in a small bowl. Beat butter, brown sugar, granulated sugar and vanilla extract in a large mixer bowl until creamy. Beat in eggs for about 2 minutes or until light and fluffy. Gradually beat in flour mixture. Stir in morsels. Drop by rounded tablespoon onto ungreased baking sheets.

BAKE for 8 to 10 minutes or until cookies are puffed. Cool on baking sheets for 2 minutes; remove to wire racks to cool completely.

Makes about 4½ dozen cookies

Triple-Chocolate Cupcakes

- **1 package (18.25 ounces) chocolate cake mix**
- **1 package (4 ounces) chocolate instant pudding and pie filling mix**
- **1 container (8 ounces) sour cream**
- **4 large eggs**
- **½ cup vegetable oil**
- **½ cup warm water**
- **2 cups (12-ounce package) NESTLÉ® TOLL HOUSE® Semi-Sweet Chocolate Morsels**
- **1 container (16 ounces) prepared frosting**
- **Assorted candy sprinkles**

PREHEAT oven to 350°F. Grease or paper-line 30 muffin cups.

COMBINE cake mix, pudding mix, sour cream, eggs, vegetable oil and water in large mixer bowl; beat on low speed just until blended. Beat on high speed for 2 minutes. Stir in morsels. Pour into prepared muffin cups, filling ⅔ full.

BAKE for 25 to 28 minutes or until wooden pick inserted in centers comes out clean. Cool in pans for 10 minutes; remove to wire racks to cool completely. Frost; decorate with candy sprinkles.

Makes 2½ dozen cupcakes

Pumpkin Apple Gingerbread Cake

       3½ cups all-purpose flour
        1 tablespoon baking powder
       2½ teaspoons ground ginger
        ½ teaspoon baking soda
        ½ teaspoon pumpkin pie spice
        ½ teaspoon salt
        1 cup (2 sticks) butter or margarine, softened
        1 cup granulated sugar
        ½ cup packed brown sugar
        4 large eggs
        1 can (15 ounces) LIBBY'S® 100% Pure Pumpkin
        1 cup (1 large) baking apple (such as Granny Smith)
          peeled, shredded
        ½ cup molasses
          Powdered sugar
          Whipped cream, vanilla ice cream or Hard Sauce
          (recipe follows)

FOR GINGERBREAD

PREHEAT oven to 350°F. Grease and flour 12-cup Bundt pan.

COMBINE flour, baking powder, ginger, baking soda, pumpkin pie spice and
   salt in medium bowl. Beat butter, granulated sugar and brown sugar in large
   mixer bowl until creamy. Beat in eggs two at a time, beating well after each
   addition. Beat in pumpkin, apple and molasses. Gradually beat in flour
   mixture.

SPOON batter into prepared Bundt pan. Bake for 55 to 60 minutes or until
   wooden pick inserted in bread comes out clean. Cool in pan on wire rack
   for 15 minutes; invert onto serving platter. Dust with powdered sugar before
   serving. Serve warm with Hard Sauce.

Makes 12 servings

Hard Sauce: *BEAT ½ cup (1 stick) softened butter and 1 teaspoon vanilla
extract in small mixer bowl until smooth. Gradually beat in 2 cups sifted
powdered sugar until fluffy.*

Oatmeal Raisin Whoopie Pies

2 packages (16.5 ounces *each*) **NESTLÉ®
TOLL HOUSE® Refrigerated Oatmeal Raisin Cookie
Bar Dough**
1 **package (8 ounces) cream cheese, at room
temperature**
4 **tablespoons butter or margarine, softened**
1 **cup powdered sugar**
1 **teaspoon vanilla extract**
½ **teaspoon ground cinnamon**

PREPARE cookies according to package directions. Cool completely.

BEAT cream cheese, butter, powdered sugar, vanilla extract and cinnamon in
small mixer bowl until smooth.

PLACE about *1 tablespoon* filling on flat side of 1 cookie; top with flat side of
second cookie to make a sandwich. Repeat with *remaining* cookies and filling.
Store in covered container in refrigerator.

Makes 2 dozen cookie sandwiches

Candy Bars

1⅔ cups (11-ounce package) NESTLÉ® TOLL HOUSE®
   Butterscotch Flavored Morsels
4 cups toasted rice cereal
2 packages (11.5 ounces *each*) NESTLÉ® TOLL HOUSE®
   Milk Chocolate Morsels, *divided*

GREASE 13×9-inch baking pan.

MICROWAVE butterscotch morsels in large, microwave-safe bowl on
MEDIUM-HIGH (70%) power for 1 minute; stir. Microwave at additional
10- to 20-second intervals, stirring until smooth. Stir in cereal and *1 cup* milk
chocolate morsels. Press evenly into prepared baking pan.

MICROWAVE *remaining* milk chocolate morsels in small, microwave-safe bowl
on MEDIUM-HIGH (70%) power for 1 minute; stir. Microwave at additional
10- to 20-second intervals, stirring until smooth. Spread evenly over mixture
in pan. Refrigerate until firm. Cut into bars.

Makes 2 dozen bars

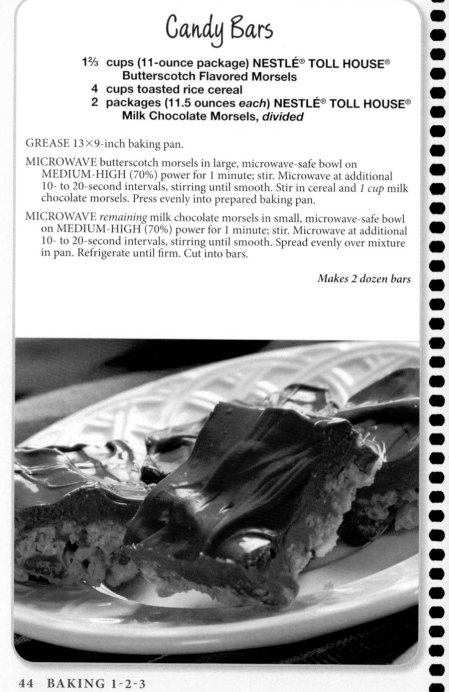

Chocolate Amaretto Bars

CRUST

2 cups all-purpose flour

¾ cup (1½ sticks) butter or margarine, cut into pieces, softened

⅓ cup packed brown sugar

FILLING

4 large eggs

¾ cup light corn syrup

¾ cup granulated sugar

2 tablespoons butter or margarine, melted

1 tablespoon cornstarch

¼ cup amaretto liqueur or ½ teaspoon almond extract

2 cups sliced almonds

2 cups (12-ounce package) NESTLÉ® TOLL HOUSE® Semi-Sweet Chocolate Morsels, *divided*

Chocolate Drizzle (recipe follows)

PREHEAT oven to 350°F. Grease 13×9-inch baking pan.

FOR CRUST

BEAT flour, butter and brown sugar in large mixer bowl until crumbly. Press into prepared baking pan.

BAKE for 12 to 15 minutes or until golden brown.

FOR FILLING

BEAT eggs, corn syrup, granulated sugar, butter, cornstarch and liqueur in medium bowl with wire whisk. Stir in almonds and *1⅔ cups* morsels. Pour over hot crust; spread evenly.

BAKE for 25 to 30 minutes or until center is set. Cool completely in pan on wire rack.

Makes about 2½ dozen bars

Chocolate Drizzle: *PLACE remaining ⅓ cup morsels in heavy-duty plastic bag. Microwave on HIGH (100%) power for 30 to 45 seconds; knead. Microwave at 10- to 15-second intervals, kneading until smooth. Cut tiny corner from bag; squeeze to drizzle over bars. Refrigerate for few minutes to firm chocolate before cutting into bars.*

Pumpkin-Oatmeal Raisin Cookies

- 2 cups all-purpose flour
- 1⅓ cups quick or old-fashioned oats
- 1 teaspoon baking soda
- 1 teaspoon ground cinnamon
- ½ teaspoon salt
- 1 cup (2 sticks) butter or margarine, softened
- 1 cup packed brown sugar
- 1 cup granulated sugar
- 1 cup LIBBY'S® 100% Pure Pumpkin
- 1 large egg
- 1 teaspoon vanilla extract
- ¾ cup chopped walnuts
- ¾ cup raisins

PREHEAT oven to 350°F. Lightly grease baking sheets.

COMBINE flour, oats, baking soda, cinnamon and salt in medium bowl. Beat butter, brown sugar and granulated sugar in large mixer bowl until light and fluffy. Add pumpkin, egg and vanilla extract; mix well. Add flour mixture; mix well. Stir in nuts and raisins. Drop by rounded tablespoons onto prepared baking sheets.

BAKE for 14 to 16 minutes or until cookies are lightly browned and set in centers. Cool on baking sheets for 2 minutes; remove to wire racks to cool completely.

Makes 4 dozen cookies

BAKING
FOR KIDS

Chocolate Oatmeal Chippers

1¼ cups all-purpose flour
½ cup NESTLÉ® TOLL HOUSE® Baking Cocoa
1 teaspoon baking soda
¼ teaspoon salt
1 cup (2 sticks) butter or margarine, softened
1 cup packed brown sugar
½ cup granulated sugar
1 teaspoon vanilla extract
2 large eggs
1¾ cups (11.5-ounce package) NESTLÉ® TOLL HOUSE®
    Milk Chocolate Morsels
1¾ cups quick or old-fashioned oats
1 cup chopped nuts (optional)

PREHEAT oven to 375°F.

COMBINE flour, cocoa, baking soda and salt in medium bowl. Beat butter, brown sugar, granulated sugar and vanilla extract in large mixer bowl until creamy. Beat in eggs. Gradually beat in flour mixture. Stir in morsels, oats and nuts. Drop dough by rounded tablespoon onto ungreased baking sheets.

BAKE for 9 to 12 minutes or until edges are set but centers are still soft. Cool on baking sheets for 2 minutes; remove to wire racks to cool completely.

Makes about 4 dozen cookies

Monster Pops

1⅔ cups all-purpose flour
1 teaspoon baking soda
½ teaspoon salt
1 cup (2 sticks) butter or margarine, softened
¾ cup granulated sugar
¾ cup packed brown sugar
2 teaspoons vanilla extract
2 large eggs
2 cups (12-ounce package) NESTLÉ® TOLL HOUSE®
  Semi-Sweet Chocolate Morsels
2 cups quick or old-fashioned oats
1 cup raisins
24 wooden craft sticks
1 container (16 ounces) prepared vanilla frosting,
  colored as desired, or colored icing in tubes

PREHEAT oven to 325°F.

COMBINE flour, baking soda and salt in small bowl. Beat butter, granulated sugar, brown sugar and vanilla extract in large mixer bowl until creamy. Beat in eggs. Gradually beat in flour mixture. Stir in morsels, oats and raisins. Drop dough by level ¼-cup measure 3 inches apart onto ungreased baking sheets. Shape into round mounds. Insert wooden stick into side of *each* mound.

BAKE for 14 to 18 minutes or until golden brown. Cool on baking sheets on wire racks for 2 minutes; remove to wire racks to cool completely.

DECORATE pops as desired. Use frosting and colored candies: WONKA® RUNTS® and/or NERDS®.

Makes about 2 dozen cookies

For Speedy Monster Pops: *SUBSTITUTE 2 packages (16.5 ounce each), NESTLÉ® TOLL HOUSE® Refrigerated Chocolate Chip Cookie Dough for the first nine ingredients, adding 1 cup quick or old-fashioned oats and ½ cup raisins to the dough. Bake as stated above for 16 to 20 minutes or until golden brown. Makes 1½ dozen cookies.*

Peanut Butter and Jelly Bars

- 1¼ cups all-purpose flour
- ½ cup graham cracker crumbs
- ½ teaspoon baking soda
- ½ teaspoon salt
- ½ cup (1 stick) butter, softened
- ½ cup granulated sugar
- ½ cup packed brown sugar
- ½ cup creamy peanut butter
- 1 large egg
- 1 teaspoon vanilla extract
- 1¾ cups (11.5-ounce package) NESTLÉ® TOLL HOUSE® Milk Chocolate Morsels
- ¾ cup coarsely chopped peanuts
- ½ cup jelly or jam

PREHEAT oven to 350°F.

COMBINE flour, graham cracker crumbs, baking soda and salt in small bowl.

BEAT butter, granulated sugar, brown sugar and peanut butter in large mixer bowl until creamy. Beat in egg and vanilla extract. Gradually beat in flour mixture. Stir in morsels and nuts. Press ¾ *dough* into ungreased 13×9-inch baking pan.

BAKE for 15 minutes; remove from oven. Dollop jelly by heaping teaspoon over partially baked dough. Let stand for 1 minute; spread to cover. Dollop *remaining* dough by heaping teaspoon over jelly.

BAKE for an additional 20 to 25 minutes or until edges are set. Cool in pan on wire rack. Cut into bars.

Makes 4 dozen bars

Scotcheroos

Nonstick cooking spray
1½ cups creamy peanut butter
1 cup granulated sugar
1 cup light corn syrup
6 cups toasted rice cereal
1⅔ cups (11-ounce package) NESTLÉ® TOLL HOUSE® Butterscotch Flavored Morsels
1 cup (6 ounces) NESTLÉ® TOLL HOUSE® Semi-Sweet Chocolate Morsels

COAT 13×9-inch baking pan with cooking spray.

COMBINE peanut butter, sugar and corn syrup in large saucepan. Cook over medium-low heat, stirring frequently, until melted. Remove from heat. Add cereal; stir until thoroughly coated. Press onto bottom of prepared baking pan.

MICROWAVE butterscotch morsels and semi-sweet chocolate morsels in large, uncovered, microwave-safe bowl on HIGH (100%) power for 1 minute; STIR. Morsels may retain some of their original shape. If necessary, microwave at additional 10- to 15-second intervals, stirring just until smooth. Spread over cereal mixture.

REFRIGERATE for 15 to 20 minutes or until topping is firm. Cut into bars.

Makes 2½ dozen bars

Polka Dot Pumpkin Cupcakes

½ cup (4 ounces) cream cheese, softened
1 large egg
2 tablespoons granulated sugar
⅔ cup **NESTLÉ® TOLL HOUSE®** Semi-Sweet Chocolate
   Mini Morsels
1 package (16 ounces) pound cake mix
1 cup **LIBBY'S®** 100% Pure Pumpkin
⅓ cup water
2 large eggs
2 teaspoons pumpkin pie spice
1 teaspoon baking soda

PREHEAT oven to 325°F. Grease or paper-line 18 muffin cups.

BEAT cream cheese, egg and granulated sugar in small mixer bowl until smooth. Stir in morsels. Set aside.

COMBINE cake mix, pumpkin, water, eggs, pumpkin pie spice and baking soda in large mixer bowl; beat on medium speed for 3 minutes. Pour batter into prepared muffin cups, filling ¾ full. Spoon about 1 tablespoon topping over batter in each muffin cup.

BAKE for 25 to 30 minutes or until wooden pick inserted in centers comes out clean. Cool in pans on wire racks for 10 minutes; remove to wire racks to cool completely.

Makes 18 cupcakes

Razz-Ma-Tazz Bars

½ **cup (1 stick) butter or margarine**
2 **cups (12-ounce package) NESTLÉ® TOLL HOUSE®
   Premier White Morsels,** *divided*
2 **large eggs**
½ **cup granulated sugar**
1 **cup all-purpose flour**
½ **teaspoon salt**
½ **teaspoon almond extract**
½ **cup seedless raspberry jam**
¼ **cup toasted sliced almonds**

PREHEAT oven to 325°F. Grease and sugar 9-inch-square baking pan.

MELT butter in medium, microwave-safe bowl on HIGH (100%) power for
   1 minute; stir. Add *1 cup* morsels; let stand. Do not stir.

BEAT eggs in large mixer bowl until foamy. Add sugar; beat until light lemon
   colored, about 5 minutes. Stir in morsel-butter mixture. Add flour, salt and
   almond extract; mix at low speed until combined. Spread ⅔ of batter into
   prepared pan.

BAKE for 15 to 17 minutes or until light golden brown around edges. Remove
   from oven to wire rack.

HEAT jam in small, microwave-safe bowl on HIGH (100%) power for 30
   seconds; stir. Spread jam over warm crust. Stir *remaining* morsels into
   remaining batter. Drop spoonfuls of batter over jam. Sprinkle with almonds.

BAKE for 25 to 30 minutes or until edges are browned. Cool completely in pan
   on wire rack. Cut into bars.

Makes 16 bars

Tip: *To sugar a baking pan, simply sprinkle it with a tablespoon of sugar
after greasing.*

Chocolate Chip Cookie Brittle

    1   cup (2 sticks) butter or margarine, softened
    1   cup granulated sugar
    1½ teaspoons vanilla extract
    1   teaspoon salt
    2   cups all-purpose flour
    2   cups (12-ounce package) NESTLÉ® TOLL HOUSE®
            Semi-Sweet Chocolate Morsels, *divided*
    1   cup chopped nuts

PREHEAT oven to 375°F.

BEAT butter, sugar, vanilla extract and salt in large mixer bowl. Gradually beat in flour. Stir in *1½ cups* morsels and nuts. Press into ungreased 15×10-inch jelly-roll pan.

BAKE for 20 to 25 minutes or until golden brown and set. Cool until just slightly warm.

MICROWAVE *remaining ½ cup* morsels in small, *heavy-duty* plastic bag on HIGH (100%) power for 30 to 45 seconds; knead. Microwave at additional 10- to 15-second intervals, kneading until smooth. Cut tiny corner from bag; squeeze to drizzle over cookie. Allow chocolate to cool and set; break cookies into irregular pieces.

Makes about 50 pieces

Note: *Including nuts helps keep these cookies moist.*

Surprise Prize Cupcakes

- 1 package (18.25 ounces) plain chocolate cake mix
- 1⅓ cup water
- 3 large eggs
- ⅓ cup vegetable oil
- 1 package (16.5 ounces) **NESTLÉ® TOLL HOUSE®** Refrigerated Chocolate Chip Cookie Bar Dough
- 1 container (16 ounces) prepared chocolate frosting **NESTLÉ® TOLL HOUSE®** Semi-Sweet Chocolate Mini Morsels

PREHEAT oven to 350°F. Paper-line 24 muffin cups.

BEAT cake mix, water, eggs and oil in large mixer bowl on low speed for 30 seconds. Beat on medium speed for 2 minutes or until smooth. Spoon about ¼ cup batter into each cup, filling about two-thirds full.

CUT cookie dough into 24 pieces; roll *each* into a ball. Place *1 ball* of dough in *each* muffin cup, pressing it into the bottom.

BAKE for 19 to 22 minutes or until top springs back when gently touched. Let stand for 15 minutes. Remove to wire rack to cool completely. Spread with frosting and sprinkle with morsels.

Makes 2 dozen cupcakes

Rich Chocolate Cake with Creamy Peanut Butter Milk Chocolate Frosting

CAKE

- 2 cups all-purpose flour
- 1¾ cups granulated sugar
- ⅔ cup NESTLÉ® TOLL HOUSE® Baking Cocoa
- 1½ teaspoons baking powder
- 1½ teaspoons baking soda
- ½ teaspoon salt
- 1 cup milk
- 1 cup water
- ½ cup vegetable oil
- 2 large eggs
- 2 teaspoons vanilla extract
- 1⅔ cups (11-ounce package) NESTLÉ® TOLL HOUSE® Peanut Butter & Milk Chocolate Morsels, *divided*

CREAMY PEANUT BUTTER MILK CHOCOLATE FROSTING

- 1 package (8 ounces) cream cheese, softened
- 1 teaspoon vanilla extract
- ⅛ teaspoon salt
- 3 cups powdered sugar

FOR CAKE

PREHEAT oven to 350°F. Grease and flour two 9-inch-round cake pans.

COMBINE flour, granulated sugar, cocoa, baking powder, baking soda and salt in large mixer bowl. Add milk, water, vegetable oil, eggs and vanilla extract; blend until moistened. Beat for 2 minutes (batter will be thin). Pour into prepared pans. Sprinkle *⅓ cup* morsels over each cake.

BAKE for 25 to 30 minutes or until wooden pick inserted in center comes out clean. Cool in pans on wire racks for 10 minutes; remove to wire racks to cool completely. Frost with Creamy Peanut Butter Milk Chocolate Frosting.

FOR CREAMY PEANUT BUTTER MILK CHOCOLATE FROSTING

MICROWAVE *remaining* morsels in small, uncovered, microwave-safe bowl on MEDIUM-HIGH (70%) power for 1 minute; STIR. Morsels may retain some of their original shape. If necessary, microwave at additional 10- to 15-second intervals, stirring just until morsels are melted. Beat cream cheese, melted morsels, vanilla extract and salt in small mixer bowl until light and fluffy. Gradually beat in powdered sugar.

Makes 12 servings

Mini Dessert Burgers

1 **box (12 ounces) vanilla wafer cookies,*** *divided*
½ **cup powdered sugar**
¼ **teaspoon salt**
¾ **cup NESTLÉ® TOLL HOUSE® Semi-Sweet Chocolate Morsels**
⅓ **cup milk**
½ **cup sweetened flaked coconut**
½ **teaspoon water**
3 **drops green food coloring**
   Red and yellow decorating gels (for ketchup and mustard)
1 **teaspoon melted butter (optional)**
1 **tablespoon sesame seeds (optional)**

*A 12-ounce box of vanilla wafers contains about 88 wafers.

RESERVE 48 wafers for bun tops and bottoms.

PLACE *remaining* wafers in large resealable bag. Crush into small pieces using a rolling pin. Combine wafer crumbs (about 1½ cups) with powdered sugar and salt in medium bowl.

MICROWAVE morsels and milk in medium, uncovered, microwave-safe bowl on HIGH (100%) power for 45 seconds; STIR. If necessary, microwave at additional 10- to 15-second intervals, stirring just until smooth.

POUR chocolate mixture into wafer mixture; stir until combined. Cool for 10 minutes. Line baking sheet with wax paper. Roll mixture into 24, 1-inch (about 1 tablespoon each) balls. Place each ball on prepared sheet;

flatten slightly to form burger patties.

COMBINE coconut, water and green food coloring in small, resealable plastic bag. Seal bag and shake to coat evenly with color.

TO ASSEMBLE

PLACE 24 wafers, rounded side down on prepared baking sheet. Top *each* wafer with 1 burger patty. Top *each* burger patty with 1 teaspoon colored coconut. Squeeze decorating gels on top of coconut. Top with *remaining* wafers. Brush tops of wafers with melted butter and sprinkle with sesame seeds, if desired.

Makes 2 dozen cookies

Tip: *Recipe can easily be doubled or tripled. Great birthday or slumber party activity.*

Cheeseburgers!: *Cut apricot fruit rollups into small ½-inch squares to create cheese for the mini burgers.*

Chunky Milk Chocolate Chip Cookies

2	cups all-purpose flour
1	teaspoon baking soda
¼	teaspoon salt
1¼	cups packed brown sugar
1	cup (2 sticks) butter or margarine, softened
1	teaspoon vanilla extract
1	large egg
1¾	cups (11.5-ounce package) NESTLÉ®
	TOLL HOUSE® Milk Chocolate Morsels
1	cup chopped nuts
1	cup raisins

PREHEAT oven to 375°F.

COMBINE flour, baking soda and salt in small bowl. Beat sugar, butter and vanilla extract in large mixer bowl until creamy. Beat in egg. Gradually beat in flour mixture. Stir in morsels, nuts and raisins. Drop by heaping tablespoon onto ungreased baking sheets; flatten slightly.

BAKE for 9 to 11 minutes or until edges are lightly browned. Cool on baking sheets for 2 minutes; remove to wire racks to cool completely.

Makes about 2½ dozen cookies

BLACK & WHITE DELIGHTS

White Fudge with Crystallized Ginger & Cranberries

- 1½ cups granulated sugar
- 1 teaspoon ground ginger
- ⅔ cup (5 fluid-ounce can) NESTLÉ® CARNATION® Evaporated Milk
- 2 tablespoons butter
- 2 cups miniature marshmallows
- 2 cups (12-ounce package) NESTLÉ® TOLL HOUSE® Premier White Morsels
- 1¼ cups (6-ounce package) sweetened dried cranberries, coarsely chopped
- 1 jar (2.5 ounces) or ½ cup crystallized ginger

LINE 8- or 9-inch-square baking pan with foil.

COMBINE sugar and ground ginger in medium, *heavy-duty* saucepan. Add evaporated milk and butter. Bring to a *full rolling boil* over medium heat, stirring constantly. Boil, stirring constantly, for 4 to 5 minutes (to 234°F). Remove from heat.

STIR in marshmallows, morsels, cranberries and crystallized ginger. Stir vigorously for 1 minute or until marshmallows are melted. Pour into prepared pan; refrigerate until firm, about 1½ hours. Lift from pan; remove foil. Cut into 48 pieces.

Makes 24 (2-piece) servings

Lemon Nut White Chip Cookies

1½ cups all-purpose flour
¾ teaspoon baking soda
½ teaspoon salt
¾ cup (1½ sticks) butter or margarine, softened
½ cup packed brown sugar
¼ cup granulated sugar
1 large egg
1 tablespoon lemon juice
2 cups (12-ounce package) NESTLÉ® TOLL HOUSE® Premier White Morsels
1 cup coarsely chopped walnuts or cashew nuts
1 teaspoon grated lemon peel

PREHEAT oven to 375°F.

COMBINE flour, baking soda and salt in small bowl. Beat butter, brown sugar and granulated sugar in large mixer bowl until creamy. Beat in egg and lemon juice; gradually beat in flour mixture. Stir in morsels, nuts and lemon peel. Drop by rounded tablespoon onto ungreased baking sheets.

BAKE for 7 to 10 minutes or until edges are lightly browned. Cool on baking sheets for 3 minutes; remove to wire racks to cool completely.

Makes about 3 dozen cookies

NESTLÉ® TOLL HOUSE® Grand Chocolate Brownie Wedges with Chocolate Sauce

3   **bars (12 ounces) NESTLÉ® TOLL HOUSE® Dark Chocolate Baking Bar,** *divided*
1   **cup granulated sugar**
⅓   **cup butter, cut into pieces**
2   **tablespoons water**
2   **large eggs**
1   **teaspoon vanilla extract**
¾   **cup all-purpose flour**
¼   **teaspoon salt**
½   **cup chopped walnuts or pecans (optional)**
⅓   **cup heavy whipping cream**
    Whipped cream (optional)

PREHEAT oven to 325°F. Line 8-inch-square baking pan with foil; grease.

HEAT *10 ounces (2½ bars)* chocolate (broken into small pieces), sugar, butter and water in small, *heavy-duty* saucepan over low heat, stirring constantly, until chocolate and butter are melted. Pour into medium bowl. Stir in eggs, one at a time, until mixed in. Stir in vanilla extract. Add flour and salt; stir well. Stir in nuts, if desired. Pour into prepared baking pan.

BAKE for 35 to 40 minutes or until wooden pick inserted in center comes out slightly sticky (may take up to 45 minutes). Cool in pan on wire rack. Lift brownie from pan with foil to cutting board. Carefully remove foil. Cut brownie square in half. Cut each half into thirds for a total of 6 pieces. Cut each piece in half diagonally to form triangles for a total of 12.

PLACE cream in small, uncovered, microwave-safe dish. Microwave on HIGH (100%) power for 25 to 30 seconds. Add *remaining 2 ounces (½ bar)* chocolate, broken into small pieces; stir until smooth. (Sauce will thicken as it cools.) Place wedge on serving plate; top or drizzle with a teaspoon of sauce. Top with whipped cream, if desired.

Makes 12 servings

White Chip Pumpkin Spice Cake

- 1 package (18.25 ounces) spice cake mix
- 3 large eggs
- 1 cup LIBBY'S® 100% Pure Pumpkin
- ⅔ cup (5 fluid-ounce can) NESTLÉ® CARNATION® Evaporated Milk
- ⅓ cup vegetable oil
- 1 cup (6 ounces) NESTLÉ® TOLL HOUSE® Premier White Morsels
  White Chip Cinnamon Glaze (recipe follows)

PREHEAT oven to 350°F. Grease and flour 12-cup Bundt pan.

COMBINE cake mix, eggs, pumpkin, evaporated milk and vegetable oil in large mixer bowl. Beat at low speed until moistened. Beat at medium speed for 2 minutes; stir in morsels. Pour into prepared Bundt pan.

BAKE for 40 to 45 minutes or until wooden pick inserted in cake comes out clean. Cool in pan on wire rack for 25 minutes; invert onto wire rack to cool completely. Drizzle *half* of glaze over cake; serve with *remaining* glaze.

Makes 16 servings

White Chip Cinnamon Glaze: *HEAT 3 tablespoons NESTLÉ® CARNATION® Evaporated Milk in small, heavy-duty saucepan over medium heat just to a boil; remove from heat. Add 1 cup (6 ounces) NESTLÉ® TOLL HOUSE® Premier White Morsels; stir until smooth. Stir in ½ teaspoon ground cinnamon. Makes about 1 cup.*

Dark Chocolate Truffles

½ cup heavy whipping cream
1⅔ cup (10-ounce package) **NESTLÉ® TOLL HOUSE®
Dark Chocolate Morsels**
**Finely chopped toasted nuts, toasted flaked coconut
and/or unsweetened cocoa powder for coating
truffles**

LINE baking sheet with parchment or wax paper.

HEAT cream to a gentle boil in medium, *heavy-duty* saucepan. Remove from
heat. Add chocolate. Stir until mixture is smooth and chocolate is melted.
Refrigerate for 15 to 20 minutes or until slightly thickened.

DROP chocolate mixture by rounded measuring teaspoon onto prepared baking
sheet. Refrigerate for 20 minutes. Shape or roll into balls; coat with nuts,
coconut or cocoa. Store in airtight container in refrigerator.

Makes about 3 dozen truffles

Decadent Chocolate Satin Pie

- 1¼ cups NESTLÉ® CARNATION® Evaporated Milk
- 2 large egg yolks
- 1⅔ cup (10-ounce package) NESTLÉ® TOLL HOUSE® Dark Chocolate Morsels
- 1 *prepared* 9-inch (6 ounces) graham cracker crust
  Sweetened whipped cream
  Chopped nuts (optional)

WHISK together evaporated milk and egg yolks in medium saucepan. Heat over medium-low heat, stirring constantly, until mixture is very hot and thickens slightly; do not boil. Place morsels in food processor fitted with metal blade. With processor running, slowly pour milk mixture into chocolate. Process 10 to 20 seconds. Scrape down sides and continue processing until smooth.

POUR into crust. Refrigerate for 3 hours or until firm. Top with sweetened whipped cream before serving; sprinkle with nuts.

Makes 8 servings

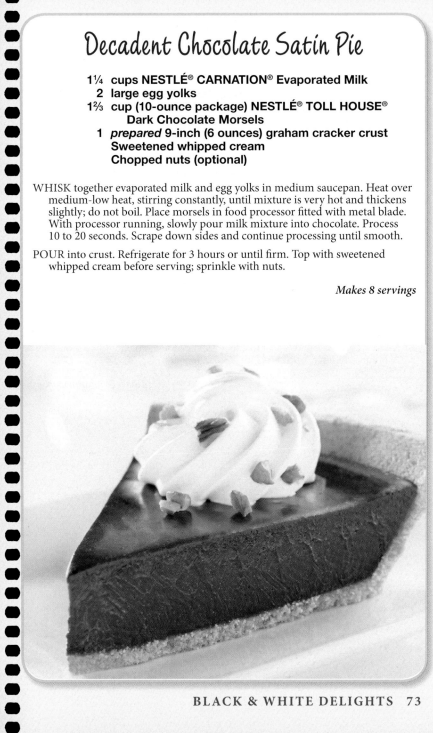

Chocolate Shortbread Olé

2 **bars (8 ounces) NESTLÉ® TOLL HOUSE® Dark Chocolate Baking Bar, broken into small pieces**
2 **cups all-purpose flour**
1 **teaspoon ground cinnamon**
⅛ **teaspoon ground cayenne pepper**
1 **cup packed light brown sugar**
¾ **cup (1½ sticks) butter, softened**
1 **cup pecans, toasted and chopped**

PREHEAT oven to 325°F.

MICROWAVE chocolate in small, uncovered, microwave-safe bowl on MEDIUM-HIGH (70%) power for 1 minute; STIR. If pieces retain some of their original shape, microwave at additional 10- to 15-second intervals, stirring just until melted. Cool to room temperature.

COMBINE flour, cinnamon and cayenne in medium bowl. Beat brown sugar and butter in large mixer bowl until light and fluffy. Beat in melted chocolate. Stir in flour mixture until blended. Stir in pecans.

SHAPE dough into 1-inch balls; place 2 inches apart on ungreased baking sheets. Flatten with bottom of glass dipped in sugar.

BAKE for 10 to 12 minutes or until edges are set. Cool on baking sheets for 2 minutes; remove to wire racks to cool completely.

Makes 3½ dozen cookies

Chocolate Peppermint Wafers

 8 ounces **NESTLÉ® TOLL HOUSE® Premier White Baking Bar, broken into small pieces**
 ⅓ **cup (about 12) coarsely crushed hard peppermint candies**
 ¾ **cup NESTLÉ® TOLL HOUSE® Semi-Sweet Chocolate Morsels**
 1 **tablespoon vegetable shortening**

LINE baking sheet with wax paper.

MICROWAVE broken baking bars in medium, uncovered, microwave-safe bowl on MEDIUM-HIGH (70%) power for 1 minute; STIR. If pieces retain some of their original shape, microwave at additional 10- to 15-second intervals, stirring until melted. Stir in candy.

SPREAD mixture to desired thickness on baking sheet. Refrigerate for 10 minutes or until firm. Break into bite-size pieces.

MICROWAVE morsels and vegetable shortening in small, uncovered, microwave-safe bowl on HIGH (100%) power for 1 minute; STIR. Morsels may retain some of their original shape. Microwave at additional 10- to 15-second intervals, stirring just until melted.

DIP candy pieces ¾ of the way into melted chocolate; shake off excess. Place back on prepared baking sheet. Refrigerate for about 15 minutes or until firm. Store in airtight container at room temperature.

Makes 10 servings
(or about ¾ pound)

Dark Chocolate Orange Fondue

⅔ cup heavy whipping cream
2 bars (8 ounces) NESTLÉ® TOLL HOUSE® Dark
    Chocolate Baking Bar, finely chopped
1 tablespoon orange liqueur (optional)
1 teaspoon grated orange peel
    Marshmallows, fresh fruit (washed and patted dry),
    cake cubes and/or pretzels

HEAT cream in small, *heavy-duty* saucepan over medium-high heat; bring just to a boil. Remove from heat. Add chocolate; stir until smooth. Add liqueur and orange peel; mix well.

TRANSFER fondue to fondue pot; place over low heat. To serve, dip marshmallows, fruit, cake and/or pretzels into melted chocolate. Stir often while on heat.

Makes 4 servings (1¼ cups total)

The Ultimate NESTLÉ® TOLL HOUSE® Chocolate Cake

CAKE

- 1½ cups granulated sugar
- 1½ cups all-purpose flour
- ¾ teaspoon baking soda
- ½ teaspoon salt
- 1 cup strong coffee
- 1½ bars (6 ounces) NESTLÉ® TOLL HOUSE® Dark Chocolate Baking Bar
- ½ cup vegetable oil
- ½ cup sour cream, room temperature
- 2 large eggs, room temperature
- 1½ teaspoons vanilla extract

FROSTING

- ⅔ cup heavy whipping cream
- 5 tablespoons unsalted butter, cut into ½-inch pieces
- 3 tablespoons granulated sugar
- 3 tablespoons water
- ⅛ teaspoon salt
- 10 ounces NESTLÉ® TOLL HOUSE® Dark Chocolate Baking Bar, finely chopped
- ½ teaspoon vanilla extract

FOR CAKE

PREHEAT oven to 325°F. Grease two 8-inch-round cake pans. Line bottoms with wax paper.

COMBINE sugar, flour, baking soda and salt in large bowl. Bring coffee to simmer in small, *heavy-duty* saucepan. Remove from heat. Add chocolate; whisk until chocolate is melted and smooth. Cool slightly.

WHISK together vegetable oil, sour cream, eggs and vanilla extract in another large bowl until blended. Add chocolate-coffee mixture; whisk to blend well. Add *one-third* of chocolate-sour cream mixture to dry ingredients; whisk to blend well. Add *remaining* chocolate-sour cream mixture in 2 more additions, whisking well after each addition. Divide batter equally between prepared pans. (Batter will be thin.)

BAKE for 33 to 35 minutes or until wooden pick inserted in centers comes out clean. Cool in pans on wire racks for 10 minutes. Run knife around edges of cakes. Invert onto wire racks; remove wax paper. Cool completely. Spread frosting between layers and over top and sides of cake. Store any leftover cake in refrigerator. Bring to room temperature before serving.

FOR FROSTING

BRING cream, butter, sugar, water and salt to simmer in medium, *heavy-duty* saucepan over medium heat, stirring frequently. Remove from heat. Immediately add chocolate; let stand for 2 minutes. Whisk until melted and smooth. Add vanilla extract. Pour into medium bowl. Refrigerate, stirring occasionally, for about 1½ hours or until thick enough to spread.

Makes 12 servings

Index